THE REALITY OF ADULTHOOD AND THE ROLLERCOASTER WITH IT

Raekwon Williams

Author's Tranquility Press
Marietta, Georgia

Copyright © 2022 by Raekwon Williams

All rights reserved. No part of this publication may be reproduced, distributed or transmitted in any form or by any means, including photocopying, recording, or other electronic or mechanical methods, without the prior written permission of the publisher, except in the case of brief quotations embodied in critical reviews and certain other noncommercial uses permitted by copyright law. For permission requests, write to the publisher, addressed "Attention: Permissions Coordinator," at the address below.

Raekwon Williams/Author's Tranquility Press
2706 Station Club Drive SW
Marietta, GA 30060
www.authorstranquilitypress.com

Ordering Information:
Quantity sales. Special discounts are available on quantity purchases by corporations, associations, and others. For details, contact the "Special Sales Department" at the address above.

The Reality of Adulthood And The Rollercoaster That Comes With It/ Raekwon Williams
Paperback: 978-1-957546-65-0
eBook: 978-1-957546-66-7

Contents

The Sweet Feeling of Wresting on That Mat 5

There's Never Enough Time 7

Growing From A Boy Into A Man 9

Money Can't Buy Happiness 10

The Real World Ain't Nice 11

It's A Struggle To Make It To The Top 13

Fight for your Career 15

Every Year Makes Me Stronger 17

The Sweet Feeling of Wresting on That Mat

*I remember stepping on a scale,
being told how much I weigh.
I remember putting on my singlet
just before my match.
I remember lacing up my shoes just
before my match.*

*I remember having to shave or cut
my nails just before my match.
I remember getting in the zone just
before my match.
I remember pacing around just
before my match.*

*But when time came to hit the mat,
the feeling was sweet.
When the time came to wrestle,
the feeling was sweet.
When the time came for the ref to
blow the whistle, the feeling was sweet.*

*It was a sweet feeling to go for a
takedown or sprawl for points
whenever the ref blew.*

*It was a sweet feeling to hear my
coaches screaming their lungs out
telling me what to do or not do.*

*It was a sweet feeling shaking hands
with my opponents whether I won
or lost.*

*The sweet feeling of wrestling on
that mat is about as sweet as*

cotton candy.

The sweet feeling of wrestling on that mat made me celebrate in victory and sometimes defeat.

The sweet feeling of wrestling on that mat taught me the principles of winning or losing.

The sweet feeling of wrestling on that mat taught me how to be a team player.

The sweet feeling of wrestling on that mat taught me the importance of sportsmanship to my opponents.

The sweet feeling of wrestling on that mat showed me that a bee won't sting unless you try to sting it.

The sweet feeling of wrestling on that mat showed me how to strike when your victim is not striking.

The sweet feeling of wrestling on that mat makes me remember why I love wrestling so much.

The sweet feeling of wrestling on that mat makes me wish that I could wrestle once again.

There's Never Enough Time

When is there time to take a prayer?
When is there time to catch your breath?
When is there time to get some sleep?
When is there time to relax and clear your mind?
When is there time to take off work?
When is there time to take off school?
When is there time to get your hair done?
When is there time to take a vacation?

When is there time to spend with family?
When is there time to spend with friends?
When is there time to fix your car?
When is there time to clean your house?

When is there time to cook a homemade dinner?
When is there time to cook at all?
When is there time to go to the gym?
When is there time to hire a personal trainer?

There's never enough time because time always flies.
There's never enough time to take a
prayer because time keeps going.
There's never enough time to catch your breath because time keeps going.
There's never enough time to sleep because time keeps going.
There's never enough time to relax because time keeps going.
Taking off work means losing money.
Taking off school means missing assignments.
Getting your hair done means losing an hour of your day.

Taking a vacation means saving money for endless months.
Spending time with family means keeping in touch.
Spending time with friends means hanging overnight.
Fixing your car means searching for countless tools.

*Cleaning your house means going upstairs to downstairs.
Cooking a homemade dinner means going step by step.
Going to the gym means going daily and not weekly.
Hiring a personal trainer means commitment.*

*There's never enough time because time always flies,
eventually your time will come to die,
but it will fly right before your very eyes.*

Growing From A Boy Into A Man

It ain't easy growing from a boy into a man.
Being a man means no longer can your parents
clean after you eat.
Being a man means you've to do your own laundry.

Being a man means no longer can
mama buy your clothes or shoes.
Being a man means paying your own bills.
Being a man means driving your own car.

Being a man means having your own privacy.
Being a man means getting your own place.
Being a man means crying when it's necessary.
Being a man means taking acceptance to your mistakes.
Being a man means handling your business.
Being a man means always being hungry for success.

Being a man means having a good judge of character.
Being a man means treating women like queens.
Being a man means knowing when to speak, and when not to.

Boys complain, but men take action.
Boys rely on others, but men are independent.
Boys blame others for their mistakes,
but men take the blame.

Boys cry over anything, but men only cry over deep things.
Boys say anything out their mouth,
but men keep their mouths sealed.

It ain't easy growing from a boy into a man
because once you're a man no longer
can your mommy or daddy hold your hands.

Money Can't Buy Happiness

Why do we sing when we have money?
Why do we dance when we have money?
Why do we showboat when we have money?
Why do we pretend to be friendly when we have money?

Why do we go to parties when we have money?
Why do we go to fancy restaurants when we have money?
Why do we buy the newest shoes when we have money?
Why do we buy the newest cars when we have money?
Why do we work less when we have money?
Why do we sleep less when we have money?
Why do we travel more when we have money?
Why do we feel entitled when we have money?

Are we really happy or is it just the money?
Have we really changed or is it just the money?
Do we need money? Yes, but money can't buy happiness.
Too much money can bring out the evils in us.
Too much money can make us greedy.
Too much money can make us conceited.
Too much money makes us forget our loved ones.

Too much money can make us violent.
Too much money can reveal our true colors.
Too much money can ruin our relationships.

We can pretend like; we live in a paradise
whenever we have money.
We can pretend to be sprinkled with joy
whenever we have money.
We can pretend to be filled with laughter
whenever we have money.

In reality, money can't buy happiness
because too much money can hurt
our spirits like it never has before.

The Real World Ain't Nice

Remember the day, you got promoted out of elementary school?
It was wonderful.

Remember the day, you escaped the depths of middle school?
It was wonderful.

Remember the day, you finally walked across that stage after 4 painful years of high school?
It was wonderful.

Remember the day, you decided to go to college?
It was wonderful.

Remember the day, you thought, you had nothing left to prove?
It was wonderful.

Remember the day that you thought all your deepest dreams were established?
It was wonderful.

Remember when you thought the real world would be easy?
Not so wonderful.

The real world ain't nice, things get harder and less easy.
The real world ain't nice, your knowledge from school must be doubled.

The real world ain't nice, you must conduct yourself more professional.

The real world ain't nice, your feelings don't matter, so kick them straight out the doors.

The real world ain't nice, your expected to behave a certain way.

*The real world ain't nice,
degrees don't make you more superior
to someone who don't have one.*

*The real world ain't nice, your judged
more based on how you walk.*

*The real world ain't nice, your judged
more based on how you talk.*

*The real world ain't nice, your expected
to pay your bills on time.*

*The real world ain't nice, if you don't pay your taxes,
the feds will come knocking at your door.*

*The real world ain't nice, if you're not paying attention,
the cops can pull you over on any given Sunday.*

*The real world ain't nice, whenever you walk those streets, you're
an opened target.*

*The real world ain't nice, be prepared to work the system.
The real world ain't nice, it's a challenge
that you may not be ready for.*

It's A Struggle To Make It To The Top

It's easy to say that you want to be something when you grow up.

It's easy to have multiple interest when you're young.
It's easy to change your mind of what you want to be as a child more than once.

Once you've a clear career path, it ain't easy.
Once you're older and have a clear mindset to where you're going, it ain't so easy.

Once your committed to that career path, it ain't so easy.

Getting to your career means taking risk.
Getting to your career means making sacrifices.
Getting to your career means saving up money.

As a child, it was easy to say you wanted to do something, but now it's time to take action.

As a child, it was easy to procrastinate, but now it's time to take action.

As a child, it was easy to change your mind, but now it's time to take action.

It's a struggle to make it to the top, it's a lonely world up there.

It's a struggle to make it to the top, your only enemy is you.

It's a struggle to make it to the top, you've got to cut back on things that you're not use to.

It's a struggle to make it to the top, you got to focus more on yourself and less on others.

*It's a struggle to make it to the top,
you got to climb your own path.*

It's a struggle to make it to the top, it may be a struggle,

but that doesn't mean that you should ever stop.

Fight for your Career

*Many of us have something that we want to be
when we grow up.
Many of us have strong visions that we may
feel is impossible to achieve.
Many of us have a gift that were unaware of.*

*Why don't we explore our gift or talent?
Why don't we build our craft now instead of later?
Why don't we build our brand while we still can?*

*We shouldn't be satisfied to settle back in second base.
We shouldn't be satisfied working endless hours
only to feel unhappy.
We shouldn't be satisfied when we've to worry
about our next paycheck.
We shouldn't have to work somewhere just
because of the money.
We shouldn't pursue a certain career just
because our parents want us too.
We shouldn't have to put on a fake smile just to
impress our boss.*

*Fight for your career, can't nobody stop you from reaching your
full potential.
Fight for your career, you should be working somewhere
because you love it, and not just because of the money.
Fight for your career, your gift will never be exposed
unless you expose it onto the world.
Fight for your career, don't let nobody tell you
what you can or can't do.
Fight for your career, ain't nothing going to get handed to you.
Fight for your career, you've got the power of your own
destiny right in the palm of your hands.*

*Fight for your career, setbacks help you grow.
Fight for your career, even when others say no.*

*Fight for your career, you will only suffer defeat if you allow it.
Fight for your career, don't be afraid to feel pain.
Fight for your career, the more you fight,
the more knowledge you will gain.
Fight for your career because nobody's going to believe in you
more than you believe in yourself.*

Every Year Makes Me Stronger

Every year makes me stronger, and every year I'm stronger.
When a new year arises, I grow older.
When a new year arises, I grow wiser.
When a new year arises, energy is brought back to my life.
When a new year arises, I feel as reset as a charged battery.
When a new year arises, I get to rewrite my wrongs.

When a new year arises, I feel like I'm more of myself and less like someone else.
When a new year arises, blossoms bloom as if the spring had come early.
When a new year arises, the air feels less moist with less rain.

When a new year arises, I can see the world more clearly.
When a new year arises, climate change feels like less of a thing.
When a new year arises, I'm as focused as a cat.

When a new year arises, I'm as fast as lighting in a bottle.
When a new year arises, I'm as smart as a chest player.
When a new year arises, only happy tears drip below my eyes.

When a new year arises, my past is thrown in the trash.
When a new year arises, I take negativity towards me with pleasure.
When a new year arises, I react more to actions and less to words.

Every year makes me stronger, and every year I'm stronger.
Every year I don't change, but every year I can take more pain.

ABOUT THE AUTHOR

I was born on December 6, 1999. I started writing stories at the age of 8, and poems at the age of 16. After growing up worrying so much about what other people thought of me and going thru depression and other problems. Poetry became my peacemaker along with already being fully attached to wrestling since I was a baby.

www.ingramcontent.com/pod-product-compliance
Lightning Source LLC
LaVergne TN
LVHW040204080526
838202LV00042B/3315